Diary of a Murder

by Terry Deary

THURSDAY 1 JANUARY

A New Year.

Time to make New Year's resolutions. I have just two . . .

1 I'm going to use this computer they bought me for Christmas to keep a diary. This diary. This very secret diary.

2 I'm going to kill my grandmother.

Nothing *personal* you understand, Gran. Normally I wouldn't hurt a fly. It's just that when you die, Gran, your money comes to me – and I can't wait for you to die. I need money now!

I leave school at Easter with no chance of a job. Jayne Clarke won't look at a boy with no money – she said so – and I want Jayne.

Sorry, Gran.

Still, it serves you right. You shouldn't be so tight with your money. You never spend any on yourself. You just sit on it and enjoy watching my greedy family running around like pet dogs. They're desperate to please you, aren't they? Hoping for a slice of that lovely money.

Nearly a million, they reckon!

And your one pleasure in life is to make them squirm and creep for every penny. Because you and I know that it's all a great big joke, don't we, Gran?

We know you changed your will and cut them all off without a brass farthing. We know you left it all to just one person.

We know you left it all to me.

Just to spite the others.

Of course you couldn't wait to enjoy the joke – you had to tell someone. You told me last September. That was a mistake. A mistake that'll cost you your life!

Can you just see their faces, Gran, when the will is read?

I can!

Of course, you'll be dead at the time. Shame.

You're a mean, cold old crow but I like you – I have your blood in me so I'm a bit like you. I think that's why you're leaving your money to me. Yes, I like you – but I like Jayne Clarke more. Jayne with her blue-velvet eyes and a voice as cool as ice-cream.

I'm going to bed now.

With luck I'll dream of Jayne.

FRIDAY 2 JANUARY

Some chance! I hardly slept at all for thinking of how I'm going to kill you, Gran. And, when I did drop off, I had nightmares. I remember one where I shot you. I pulled the trigger, heard the bang . . . then watched you sit up, grin and scream, "You missed, Tony lad! You'll have to do better than that!"

And you were right! I'll have to do better than that. I can't afford to fail. They'd lock me away and you'd cut me out of your will. So how do I do it AND get away with it? I've had a sleepless night to think about it.

What about an accident? You know the sort of thing . . . cut the brake cable on your car so it runs away out of control. Looks good at the cinema – but you'd probably hit your gate-post at five miles an hour, bruise your big toe and come out screaming blue murder.

I could poison you – but where would I get the poison? Pop into Boots? Imagine it!

"Excuse me. Please would you sell me a bottle of poison? It must have no taste, no smell and be as deadly as my dad's socks!"

"Certainly, son. Is it for rats?" the chemist will ask.

"No. It's for my granny."

"Oh! You should have said. In that case you want a bottle of 'Granny-gon'," he'll say. "Use it myself on all my grannies. Works a treat!"

No. It can't be that easy or the family would have poisoned you years ago, you mean old bat.

I could strangle you. But you're a tough old boot and I'm a bit weedy – as my mother is always telling me.

What if you don't want to die yet, Gran? What if you struggle? Can I say, "Hold still, Gran, while I get this rope round your scrawny neck!"? No, no. But I'm going to get you somehow. Some way.

We're coming round to your house this Sunday for tea. Maybe I'll get some ideas then.

SATURDAY 3 JANUARY

Shopping this morning. Bought new games for this computer. Funny, that. Mum and Dad bought me this computer to play games on. But I found this electronic diary program. Yes, this one I'm working on now. Somehow it's much more interesting.

Funny, because I've always hated English lessons at school. I can't spell. This computer does that for me. But they'd never let me take the computer to school.

Of course, the English teacher hates me. That doesn't help.

While I was out shopping I went into the "Country Sports" shop in town. Shotguns cost a thousand quid. If I save every penny of my five pounds a week pocket money I'll be able to buy one in about four years' time.

There has to be a quicker way.

I wanted to phone Jayne this afternoon – and ask her out tonight.

But I'm too scared she might say no. We got on well enough at the school Christmas disco. We danced. "Take you home later?" I asked.

She laughed. "I only go home with men, not boys!"

You always hurt the one you love, they say. She must be crazy about me.

"So, you'll go home with me when I'm a man?"

"I can't wait fifty years," she joked. "Anyway, my man would have to have a car to take me home. A fast, expensive car."

"I'll have one soon," I promised.

That made her look at me more closely. "You?"

"Yes. You'll see!" I said.

"Where would a creep like you get the money? Steal it?"

"I'll have a million soon," I told her.

She laughed again – but not so loudly this time. I could see she was interested. "You can take me home for – for a thousand," she said softly.

"It's a deal!" I said.

But I can't phone her just yet. I don't have that thousand – yet. I'll see her next week at school. But, before then, I want to finish my plan for Gran – my "Gran Plan".

School starts a week Monday – 12th January.

I have nine days.

SUNDAY 4 JANUARY

I hate Gran's house. It's tall and dark, hidden behind high hedges and a wild garden.

"Hire a gardener," Dad told her.

"Gardeners cost money. Why should I hire men to work when I have fit and healthy children and grandchildren to help me?" Gran sneered.

Dad was round the next day cutting her grass. He'd have cut it with a pair of scissors if he thought it would get him a gold star from Gran.

Dad's worse at gardening than he is at being a father. A total failure. Now Gran has a lawn with a bald patch in the middle and a pile of dead cuttings round the outside.

But the house is even gloomier inside.

Dark oak panels cover the walls and brown velvet curtains hang at the dusty windows.

"Hello, Gran!" I said brightly.

She looked at me sharply. Could she read my mind? See the plans I have for her? "Hello, Tony," she said at last. Then she gave me that smile.

The smile that could kill a cat.

She always serves tea in the best china cups – and I'll swear those dusty cakes were the ones left over from last week.

Nobody ever speaks unless Gran speaks to them first.

"How are things at the factory, Edward?" she asked Dad, as usual.

"Fine, Mother, fine!" he mumbled. Gran knows when he's lying. He rubs the bald spot on his head – bald as the patch on Gran's lawn.

He didn't dare tell her about the strike in

the packing department. Gran owns the factory. She can sack Dad any time she wants.

"Good," Gran said with an evil smile. "I'll pop in tomorrow and see for myself."

A look of panic flashed across Dad's face. He tried to smile and muttered weakly, "Fine, Mother, fine."

But in the car, coming home, he hissed, "I wish she were dead!"

You're not alone, Dad.

I'll see what I can do!

MONDAY 5 JANUARY

Went to the library today.

They don't have books on "How to kill your gran and get away with it." But they do have detective stories. I skimmed through a few. They were no use.

In the books the police are always stupid. Some private detective finds the killer . . . but not until another six people have died.

Then I came across some true-life murder cases. The trouble is, of course, they only tell about the murderers who got caught. Still I learned some mistakes to avoid, like:

1. The killer is usually the most obvious person – in Gran's case that could be anyone in our family.

2. The killer always has a good reason – "motive" they call it. I have one million good reasons . . . one million pounds!
3. The killer always leaves clues. Fingerprints or footprints or traces of blood on his clothes. Or the police find out where he got the poison or the gun or the knife. They even find out where he hid it afterwards.
4. The killer can't prove he was somewhere else at the time of the crime. To get away with it you need something called an "alibi".

I can't afford to make even one of those mistakes. Yet I nearly made my first one there and then! I was just about to take the murder book out of the library when it hit me.

Imagine, one week from now.

Gran's murder all over the front pages of

the local paper. The librarian reads it and says, "But her grandson was in here last week . . . reading a book about famous murderers!"

"Aha!" says Chief Inspector Plod. "We'll have to look closely at that young man's story!"

I felt faint at the thought. I pushed the murder book back and snatched the first book to hand without looking at the title.

The librarian will still remember me, though.

Not many sixteen-year-old boys read *The Healthy Baby Book.*

I don't even like babies.

TUESDAY 6 JANUARY

Another bad night's sleep.

That mistake with the library book shook me. It taught me that this is not going to be as easy as I thought.

Even this diary could be a mistake!

The police will find it, no matter where I hide it. There was a case last year where a kidnapper kept a computer diary of his crime. He thought he'd wiped it off his disc – but the experts used some electronic device to read that diary.

Of course they did that after he was arrested. They will only find this diary if they look . . . and they'll only start looking if they suspect me.

I have to have this diary, though. It helps

me get my thoughts straight. I can't very well talk the plan over with anybody, can I? I have to do this alone . . . don't I?

I know Dad wants the old trout dead. Can I say to him, "I'm going to cut Gran's throat tonight, Dad. If the police ask where I was, tell them I was with you all night."

"Yes, son! Go ahead!"

Let me think about it.

Q.1 Would the police believe Dad?

A Maybe not. After all, he'll be one of the chief suspects himself.

Q.2 Would Dad lie for me?

A Probably. He wouldn't have the guts to cut Gran's throat himself, but he may be so grateful he'd be prepared to lie about it. Of course Dad's not a good liar. He'd start rubbing his bald patch and give himself away.

Q.3 Can I trust Dad to keep quiet?

A Yes . . . but hang on! No! Once the will is read (and Dad finds out I get all of Gran's money) he'll be furious. He'll be hammering at Chief Inspector Plod's door. *"My son did it! He did it for the money! Come and take the little swine away!"*

No! Forget that idea. I can't bring Dad in on my plan.

Still, there's something there. A half idea at the back of my mind. I'll sleep on it. Maybe things will seem clearer tomorrow.

But I'll have to hurry. Only six days to go.

WEDNESDAY 7 JANUARY

What a day! Dad came in from work looking as if someone had stepped on his corns!

"Gran was at the factory today," he said.

"Oh," Mum said.

There was no need to say anything else, really. It was after tea that Dad dropped the real bombshell. "She found out about the strike in the packing department."

"She would," Mum muttered.

Dad took a deep breath. "She said she wants to sort it all out herself."

"But you're the manager," Mum whined. "What will the workers think?" she asked.

"They'll think we're going on holiday."

"But we're not!" Mum sighed.

"We are," Dad said quietly. "We're

booked to go to the Canary Islands tomorrow. Gran arranged it."

Mum just gaped.

"Great!" I cried.

"You're not going!" Dad said sharply. "You start school again in five days. Your last term. It's important."

I shrugged. That suited me. But I wasn't expecting what came next.

"You'll stay with your Gran," Dad said. "It's all been fixed up."

Oh, Jayne, is this Fate taking a hand or what? It was Fate that put us in the same school. Fate that made you fall for me. Fate is sending me to Gran's house. Now Fate is giving me the hammer to knock down the only wall between us – the money.

Talking about hammers makes me wonder. A hammer is a dangerous weapon in the wrong hands.

TUESDAY 8 JANUARY

Here I am . . . at the victim's house.

First chance I've had to look it over properly since I decided to get rid of Gran. That's something all good criminals do. Get to know the layout. They call it "casing the joint" in the detective books.

Gran sleeps in the middle room at the front of the first floor.

I sleep at the back with just the garden sounds for company. It's a small room. Used to belong to a servant, Gran said.

She also said that Grandad died in the room next door. Charming.

"Does he haunt it?" I asked.

"Don't be stupid, boy!" she said.

Fair enough.

At least I've got this computer for company.

Now I'm shivering as I try to write this. Hail is rattling on the window – or it could be Grandad, I suppose. Stay out there, old man! You're better off. Probably a lot warmer! Gran's too mean to have central heating.

It'll be hot enough where you're going, Gran. Soon. Soon.

And I'm hungry. Gran expects me to cook for myself. Me! Cook! Mum once told a friend, "Tony's the only boy I know who can burn a boiled egg!"

And in Food Technology lessons in school I always skipped the cookery parts of the course. The Cookery teacher hates me anyway. Cookery and games. I hate games. Except computer games, of course.

They're so clever, my computer games. Always finding new ways to kill the enemy.

I was in the kitchen earlier this evening, looking for some food I couldn't burn. I found the axe Gran uses for fire-wood. She was sitting at the kitchen table. I was standing behind her, testing the axe edge.

"Fancy a chop?" she said suddenly.

I nearly choked. I dropped the axe with a clatter.

"What are you doing, stupid boy? I asked you if you fancied a chop. There's a lamb chop in the freezer and a frying pan in the cupboard."

"I can't cook," I said.

"You'll soon learn, or you'll go hungry," she said with that wicked smile.

The chop was raw and bloody when I ate it. I'm hungry, I'm cold.

I hate you, Gran. You'll be sorry.

Four days till I see Jayne.

FRIDAY 9 JANUARY

I've got it!

I know how to kill her and get away with it! The idea began with some strange dreams I had last night.

The ghost of Grandad came back. He chopped Gran up and put her in the frying pan. Thank you, Grandad's ghost! You showed me the way to do it!

For, in my dream, I let you kill her. That's the answer! I'll get someone else to kill her!

I know there are men who kill for money. I don't suppose they put adverts in the Yellow Pages.

Got a Granny?

Want to get rid of her?
Hire a killer from

KILLAGRAN LTD

Quick, clean and cheap!
(Special rates for two or more!)

No, they won't advertise. But they must be out there. I just have to find them.

The money might be a problem. I can't pay until after Gran's dead and I've got her money. But the killer will probably want paying before he does the job.

Still, I can worry about that when I've found him. I'll start looking tomorrow night at The Bat Cave – a pub in Easinglea. A lot of roughs go there.

Some of the boys from school go in there to drink. They're under age, of course, but they look eighteen. I don't. I look about thirteen. And I don't dress like them. And my hair isn't cut like theirs. I'm too clean to be one of them. That's why they hate me.

I don't care. When I'm rich I'll dress the way I want and I'll have all the friends I want. Not that I want any. I just need one. Jayne.

Two days until I see her.

SATURDAY 10 JANUARY

I've seen her! I've seen Jayne.

I went to The Bat Cave as I planned. It's so dark and smoky in there that no one can see how old you are.

And it smells. It smells of stale beer and cigarette smoke. The smell hangs around the thick black curtains.

It's got plastic bats hanging from the ceiling. Toilets marked 'Hiss' and 'Hearse'. Somebody must have bust a gut laughing at that one.

The walls were decorated to look like a dungeon with scenes from Dracula which glowed in the ultra-violet light.

And the noise was deafening. Music from the jukebox turned up full. People shouting to be heard over the top of that noise.

I'll bet there were fifty people in there drinking under age. I sat in the darkest corner. A group burst through the door. I could hear their laughing and singing over the blast of the jukebox.

It was some sort of a party. And, in the middle of the group, there was a boy. My age . . . but twice my size.

Mickey Taylor.

He was in my class at school – until he started getting into trouble. They locked him away and I haven't seen him for years.

I edged closer. It seemed to be a party to celebrate Mickey getting out of the remand home. The girls swirled round him like butterflies – but one in a silver dress fluttered away and sat at the end of the bar near me.

"Jayne!" I cried.

She peered at my face through the murk.

"Hello," she smiled. "It's the boy who'll give a thousand pounds to take me home! Got the thousand yet, love?"

"Soon, Jayne, soon! Er . . . buy you a drink?"

"Brandy and Babycham."

I bought it, she took it. I didn't see her again for the rest of the evening.

But I've made contact. That's the main thing.

She'll remember me.

Hope I dream about her.

SUNDAY 11 JANUARY

Started off a boring day. Ended up very exciting!

My plan is taking shape.

Gran had me out in the garden, raking up dead leaves. I was very cold, but she wouldn't let me come in until lunch. We nibbled on a scrawny chicken and chewed roast potatoes that were raw in the middle. And Mum calls *me* a bad cook!

I'd just finished when there was a knock on the kitchen door.

"Paper boy!" Gran said.

"That'll be one pound fifty, Mrs Robson," the boy said.

"Wait!" Gran snapped. "I'll get the money."

She dumped the papers on the kitchen table and marched into the hall. I suddenly wondered where she kept her money. I slipped out after her.

The kitchen door creaked, but she didn't seem to hear. I watched her enter the library. I could see her through the crack in the door.

Gran took out a heavy, red book and opened it. The book was hollow! And it was full of cash!

She took some out and put the book away. I hurried into the kitchen and pretended that I'd been reading the Sunday paper. Gran paid the boy and went back to her peaches and custard.

But tonight, when Gran was asleep, I crept downstairs and found the book. It was stuffed with money! I counted it quickly – then I counted it slowly. Nine hundred and eighty-three pounds!

Now I know who will kill Gran.

And I know how I'll pay him.

Goodnight, Gran. Goodnight Grandad's ghost.

School – and Jayne – tomorrow.

MONDAY 12 JANUARY

I saw Mickey Taylor in the yard this morning at break. He was smoking, but none of the duty teachers dared to stop him.

And none of the kids dared to talk to him.

"Hello, Mickey," I said smiling.

He ignored me.

"I'm Tony Robson, remember?" He threw his cigarette end at my feet. "How would you like to earn a thousand quid?" I asked.

He looked at me as if he was seeing me for the first time. "Robson? You the kid with the rich Grandmother?"

I nodded.

"Get away from me!" he said in a low, vicious voice. I took a step back, afraid. "When you want to talk business with me make sure there's no one else around," he growled.

"Tonight, after school?" I said.

"Half-four. Back lane behind the school. Now get lost."

I got lost.

By half-past four it was cold and dark. I was scared. When my watch said 4:40 I turned to go home. A shadow stepped out of the black bushes and blocked my way.

"How do I get this thousand quid?" the figure asked. It was Mickey Taylor.

I swallowed and found my voice. "My Gran keeps that much in her house. I know exactly where."

"You'd want half, I suppose," he said. He pulled the lapels of my coat till his face was next to mine. I could smell the cigarette smoke on his breath.

I shook my head.

"So, what do you get out of it?" he asked.

"If you kill her during the robbery then I get to inherit a million pounds."

Even in the dark I saw his eyes glitter.

It was a mistake saying that bit about a million pounds.

TUESDAY 13 JANUARY

The Thirteenth today. Unlucky for some. Unlucky for you, Gran. You have just three days left to live.

You die on Friday 16th January. It's settled.

Mum and Dad will be back on Wednesday. Tomorrow will be my last night in your cold, grotty house.

On Friday I'll be in The Bat Cave and there'll be fifty witnesses to say that I'm there at the time you die. I'll have my "alibi".

Want to know who'll kill you, Gran? His name is Mickey Taylor.

Mickey wants another thousand pounds after he kills you. I'll pay him out of your money, Gran. The money I'll get when you die.

Want to know how he'll do it? He'll get into your house on Friday night – hope you don't mind, Gran, but I loaned him your house key to have a copy made.

He'll go straight to your room – I've drawn him a plan. He'll make it look as if you caught a burglar and the burglar killed you. (I don't know quite how he'll do it . . . I don't really want to know the details.)

Then he'll take the money and wreck the library to make it look as if he had to search.

Simple. Foolproof. And worth it, Gran. Yes, really worth it, Gran. I know because a strange thing happened at school today.

Jayne talked to me.

"Hello, Tony," she said in the corridor beside the sports hall.

"Tony"! Get that? Not "Creep" or "Boy". But "Tony".

"Hello, Jayne," I said. And then I couldn't

think of anything else to say. You get days like that.

"Got that thousand pounds yet, Tony?" she asked and slipped an arm around my neck.

"Yes . . . no . . . soon!" I said stupidly.

She breathed close to my ear and I could smell her perfume. I thought about fainting – and then decided it might put her off me. "I can't wait, Tony," she whispered. "I'll be in The Bat Cave, Friday night," she added.

So will I, Jayne. So will I!

Oh, yes, Gran. You won't be dying for nothing. Jayne loves me.

WEDNESDAY 14 JANUARY

Mum and Dad back home.

I won't have to stay in that haunted room any longer.

Sorry, Grandad. Nothing against you personally – still, you'll have Gran's ghost for company on Friday night. Imagine it!

You'll say, "Hello, Grandma! What are you doing here?" Then you'll act surprised. Pretend you didn't know about my little plot.

"I've just been murdered, you old fool," she'll say.

"That'll explain the axe in your head, my dear," you'll tell her.

"Of course that explains the axe in my head. What else could explain it?" she'll ask.

"It could be a new hat," you'll say.

"I wouldn't pick a hat like this," she'll say. "It doesn't even suit me!"

"I don't know," you can tell her. "That red trickle of blood down your forehead matches your lipstick perfectly!"

"Stop babbling and show me the way to Heaven, you old fool," she'll snap.

That's when you'll smile softly and say, "Oh, but dearest, didn't you know? You won't be going to Heaven!"

"Oh, hell!" she'll swear.

"Exactly," you'll say.

Bye, Grandad.

Mickey Taylor gave me back Gran's key today. He has a copy.

And Jayne smiled at me and winked. She's crazy about me!

THURSDAY 15 JANUARY

Everything's ready. I think.

I called on Gran on the way to school. "Here's your key back, Gran," I said.

"Thank you, Anthony," she smiled. "We don't want it to get into the wrong hands, do we?" she added. Why did she say that? Does she know?

"Goodbye, Gran," I said softly. Not good-night or see-you-later. Goodbye! I turned to go.

"Wait!" she said suddenly. I went cold. She does know! Perhaps she really is a witch! She's read my mind! I turned back.

"When do you leave that awful school?" she asked.

"Easter!" I said.

"Have you got a job to go to?"

"Fat chance," I said. "I won't pass any exams. The teachers will make sure of that. They hate me!"

"Come and see me, when you leave. You can start at the factory. A clever lad like you can go all the way to the top. You'd have to work hard, but in ten years you could have your father's job as manager. Smart lad like you."

"I'll think about it," I promised.

You're right. I am smart. Too smart to slave for ten years only to end up like Dad. Going bald with worry. Jayne wouldn't like that. When we're married we'll live in the best house and have the best car in the town. When I get rid of you, Gran, I'll own the factory. Why would I want to work?

And Dad can keep his job – but he'll be working for me! I like that idea.

"Clean my boots, Dad."

"Yes, son."

"And don't call me 'son'. Call me 'sir'!"

"Yes, sir!"

Now that's what I call smart!

FRIDAY 16 JANUARY

Twelve midnight.

I wonder if she's dead yet. She always goes to bed at half-past ten, after the television news. I told Mickey to go into her house at a quarter to eleven. At that time tonight I was in The Bat Cave – I was half-drunk, making a noise and making sure that people took notice of me.

Mickey should have gone through the back door and up the stairs. Did he, Gran? What did you say to him?

"Hello, lad, can I help you?"

"Yes, missis. You can tell me where you keep your money."

"In the bank."

"Funny beggar. I mean your cash!"

"In my piggy bank."

"And where's your piggy bank?"

"I keep it under my pillow."

"Would you like to pass it out?"

"Say 'please', young man."

"Would you like to pass it out, please?"

"No."

"No?"

"No!"

"But I want it!"

"You'll just have to wait, sonny."

"I said 'please'!"

"And I said 'no', so take a hint and get out!"

"Well, if you won't give me the money, I'll just have to take it."

"I won't let you."

"Then I'll just have to hit you on the head with this axe, missis!"

And then you reach under your pillow,

don't you, Gran? And what do you pull out, Gran? It's not a piggy bank, is it? No. It's that Luger pistol that Grandad brought back from the war.

Sorry, Mickey. I didn't tell you that Gran keeps a pistol under her pillow.

I didn't want to put you off.

SATURDAY 17 JANUARY

"You stupid little nerd," Mickey Taylor said on the phone this morning.

He said some other rude words including several I'd never heard before. The computer spell-checker didn't know them either. They don't put words like that in spell-checkers.

"What's wrong, Mickey?" I asked when he stopped for breath.

"You didn't tell me about the gun, you little creep, that's what's wrong!"

"But did you kill her?" I asked.

"Kill her! I'm lucky she didn't kill me! She pulled out this bloody big gun and said she'd blow my head off! I nearly peed myself!"

"You could have got the gun off her," I

told him. "She's only an old woman."

"And I'm only John bloody Wayne!" he screamed. "I nearly dropped the money."

"You got the money, then?" I asked.

"Yes."

"What about my share?" I reminded him.

"What share?" he breathed. He sounded nasty.

"I told you where the money was . . ."

"The money was for me," Mickey snarled.

"Only if you killed Gran," I said calmly.

"I took all the risks!" he said. His voice began to rise again. "She saw me!" he yelled.

"But she won't know who you are . . . unless I tell her."

There was a long, long silence.

"I'll give you a hundred," he said at last.

"Five hundred," I said.

Another long silence. "Right," he breathed. "After school, Monday night, same place." Then the phone went dead.

That's when Mum walked into the room. "Who were you talking to?"

"John bloody Wayne," I said.

The phone rang. Mum picked it up. She listened. She gave a dramatic cry of horror. "No!"

She covered the mouthpiece and turned to me. "Somebody tried to murder your gran last night."

"Makes a change from her trying to murder someone with her cooking," I said before I walked out.

I was thinking about what I'd say to Mickey when I saw him on Monday.

But I didn't have to wait till Monday to see him again. I saw him tonight in The Bat Cave. He was spending money like water – my money – and Jayne Clarke was fluttering round him like a moth round a candle flame.

I hate him.

SUNDAY 18 JANUARY

Gran is really enjoying herself.

Front page news in the local Sunday papers – queues of reporters wanting to talk to her.

GUN-TOTING GRANNY BLASTS BEDROOM BURGLAR!

one headline said.

Sharp shooting saved my skin, says Supergran!

another claimed.

The papers forgot to say that she didn't even fire the gun.

"I would have shot him right between the eyes!" Gran said when we went for tea.

"Oh, Mother, you wouldn't!" my mum gasped.

"I would," Gran said and her mouth was like a fly-trap plant.

"Pity you didn't," Dad said grimly.

Pity you didn't, I thought.

"Why didn't you?" my mum said.

"I tried . . . but I didn't know the safety catch was on!" Gran growled.

"Pity," Dad sighed.

"And the police made a fuss about me having no licence for that gun!" Gran sniffed. "More fuss than they made about my money! I think they'd rather have seen me murdered in my bed!"

"Oh, Gran!" Mum moaned.

"The police wanted to take my gun away from me – but when they found it was too rusty to work anyway they let me keep it. I'll use it to scare the next young villain off."

"The next!" Dad choked. "If you think there'll be others then you should have better locks fitted."

Gran took a deep breath and looked around the table. "The best locks in the world won't work when the thief has a key."

I nearly choked on a stale cream bun.

"Surely not, Mother!" my mum gasped.

Gran smiled smugly. "And when the police find out where he got that key from then they'll find out who he is." Her cat-green eyes turned towards me. I could hardly breathe as she said. "And how did he know where I keep my money?"

She knows! The old crow knows!

But she can't prove it. Can she?

I am safe.

Aren't I?

MONDAY 19 JANUARY

I could kill Mickey Taylor.

He's got my money and he's got my girl. He was wearing a new leather jacket at school today. "Hundred and ninety quid it cost me," he was boasting. Jayne Clarke will wear out the sleeve if she keeps clinging to it like that.

"Got a thousand quid to take me home?" she asked with a smile. She knows I haven't. She knows Mickey has . . . and I bet she knows where he got it from. That's why she's laughing at me. I've just set it up so that her boyfriend could make an easy thousand quid.

I don't get Gran's million – I don't even get her thousand cash – and I don't get Jayne.

I wish they were both dead.

There is just one chance left for me. I met Mickey Taylor in the back street after school.

"Where's my five hundred?" I asked.

"You'll have to earn it," he said.

"I'll tell the police if you don't hand it over. Gran will recognize you and you'll go back to the remand home," I told him.

I expected him to get angry. He laughed. "If I go back inside I'll take you with me. I'll tell them who gave me the key." I had no answer to that so he went on, "We'll do a deal."

"What deal?" I said.

"You get your Granny's wood-axe for me and I'll pay you five hundred pounds."

"Why?"

He sighed. "I took it up to her bedroom. When I ran off I dropped it in the kitchen log basket. Sooner or later she'll remember that I had it in my hand and she'll tell the police. They'll test it for fingerprints – and then I've had it."

"Give me the five hundred and I'll get it."

His teeth shone like a wolf's in the pale lamplight. "Get it . . . and then I'll hand over the five hundred."

I gave in and agreed. I hate him.

I'll get the rotten axe. But if he doesn't pay me then I'll be a bit upset.

But how do I get the axe. Ask her?

"Hello, Gran. Just come to borrow your axe."

"What for?"

"My pet giraffe needs its fringe chopping."

"Are you telling me the truth, Tony?"

"No. That's just a tall story."

TUESDAY 20 JANUARY

Gran suspects.

Guess who she suspects?

You'd be wrong!

"Hello, Gran," I said with a smile when I went round earlier tonight. "Dad was worried about you so I called round to see if . . ."

She stuck a bony claw into my shoulder and dragged me into the kitchen. "Come in! Come in!" She sat at the table and fixed her diamond-hard eyes on me. "Your dad isn't worried about me! He wants to see me dead!"

I gasped. I almost laughed.

"He wants to own the factory. He doesn't want me telling him how to run it."

"But what makes you think he wants to kill you?"

"The key . . . and the money!" I tried hard to look blank. I felt sick.

"Who else had a chance to have the key copied?" she asked. "And who else knew where I kept my money?"

"Money?" I tried to sound stupid.

She lowered her eyes. "I used to keep a little bit of money in the house," she said. "And the thief went straight to it! Only your dad knew where that money was kept. It was your Grandad's hiding place years ago."

"But why would he tell the thief where to find your money?" I asked.

"Payment!" Gran hissed. "The thief was to get the money in payment for killing me!"

You hit the nail on the head there, Gran, I thought.

"But he didn't kill you," I pointed out.

"No – but that was only because I had the

gun," Gran said. "He *meant* to kill me. You don't rob a house with a hatchet in your hand!"

"Hatchet!" I think I jumped a metre off the chair.

"Axe! He had a big log axe!" She turned to her log basket and pointed. "Like that one but twice as big!"

Sweat was trickling down from my armpits. Even Gran can make mistakes. "You didn't tell the police, did you?"

She leaned forward. "I hate your father, Tony," she said. "But I don't want the shame of him going to prison. I want him to own up. To confess. To put it in writing. His confession will go to my lawyers. If I die with an axe in my head then he'll go to prison for life. Once I get him to confess I'll be safe!"

I nodded numbly. Gran went to make a cup of coffee.

I can't pinch her axe now. But I did get a good close look at it. Later this evening I went to the town centre and bought one just the same.

Thick Mickey Taylor will never know the difference.

WEDNESDAY 21 JANUARY

It's all over.

Mickey got the axe – and I got my five hundred pounds.

A lot of good they'll do either of us now.

This is what happened. I kept the axe in my school bag all day. Snow was falling as I waited in the dark back lane at half-four. For once Mickey wasn't late.

"Got the axe?" he said.

"Got the money?" I asked.

He waved a handful of notes at me. "Axe first," he said.

"Money," I said quietly.

He smiled and slowly shook his head. Suddenly I became angry. Furious. Mad . . . and I mean insane. I snatched the axe from my bag and began to wave it at him. “Give me the money, Taylor!”

“Or what?” he sneered.

“Or I’ll kill you!” I choked. I was hardly able to speak.

He threw his head back and laughed. Suddenly he made a grab for the axe. I pulled it out of his reach.

I brought it down sharply to knock his hand away. I’ll swear that’s all I meant to do! But he was moving too fast. He was too close. I missed his hand. The axe caught him on the side of the head.

“That’s done it,” I thought. That’ll make him angry. He’ll kill me.

I closed my eyes. I waited for his hard fists.

Nothing.

I opened my eyes. Mickey was standing in the snow with a stupid look on his face. He swayed towards me. He swayed away from me. His eyes closed. He fell against me and slid gently to the ground.

I snatched the money from his rigid fingers. I tore some of it. I dropped the axe and ran.

It was on the late news on television tonight. Brutal murder – savage axe attack – police warning people to stay off the streets – body found by his pretty teenage girlfriend – Jayne Clarke.

I watched the screen. I sighed, "But I only tapped him! Just a little tap!"

So Mickey got the axe.

And I got my five hundred pounds – five hundred and thirty five to be exact.

Not that it will do me much good.

They'll find my fingerprints on that axe.

They'll find hundreds of my footprints in the snow.

They'll find the scraps of five-pound notes to match the torn ones in my room.

They'll find Mickey's blood on my clothes.

They'll find the shopkeeper I bought the axe from.

All the mistakes I swore I wouldn't make.

And Jayne will tell them where to find me.

They're knocking on the front door now.

I'm so tired now. Drained. Exhausted.

This began as a diary of a murder – it's that all right.

But it didn't quite work out the way I meant it. I don't get Gran's money . . . and I don't get Jayne Clarke . . . yet. Next time I'll do the job myself. I'll finish Gran off just like I finished Mickey Taylor.

There are voices downstairs.

And when I get out of prison I'll be somebody. They'll still hate me – but they'll fear me. I'll have a dozen girls like Jayne

Clarke.

There are footsteps on the stairs.

I never wanted Jayne anyway. All I ever wanted was my computer. My games.

The door's locked. If they want to come in they'll have to break it down.

Why can't they just leave me alone? Go away!

Will they let me take the computer into prison?

Maybe not. They hate me.

Leave me alone!

But when I get out I'll start this diary again. Next time I'll get it right.

Goodbye . . . for now.

END